TEENS IN THAILAND

Teens in Thailand

Thailand

by Sandy Donovan

Content Adviser: Grant Olson,
Coordinator of Information Technology,
Department of Foreign Languages &
Literatures, Northern Illinois University

Reading Adviser: Alexa L. Sandmann, Ed.D.,
Professor of Literacy, College and
Graduate School of Education, Health,
and Human Services, Kent State University

Compass Point Books ✦ Minneapolis, Minnesota

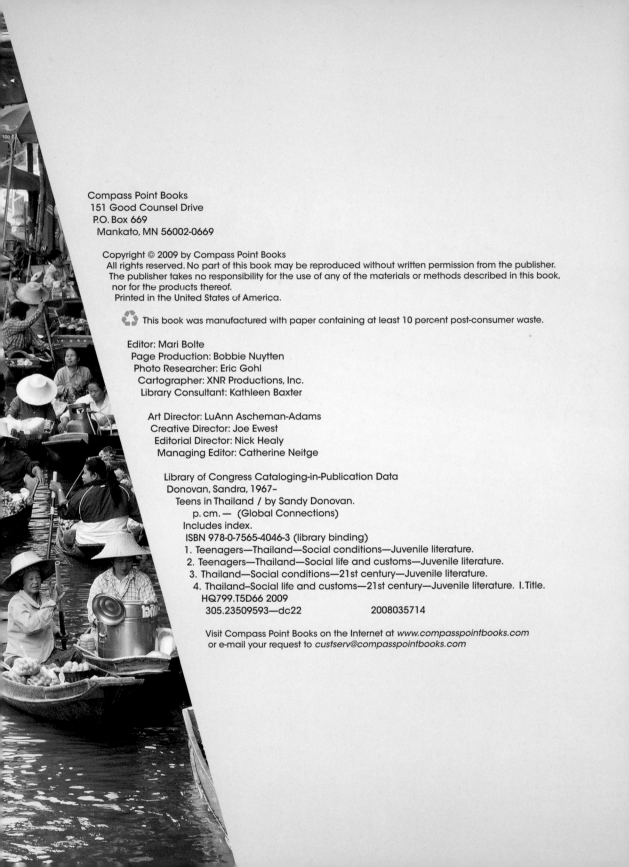

Compass Point Books
151 Good Counsel Drive
P.O. Box 669
Mankato, MN 56002-0669

This book was manufactured with paper containing at least 10 percent post-consumer waste.

Editor: Mari Bolte
Page Production: Bobbie Nuytten
Photo Researcher: Eric Gohl
Cartographer: XNR Productions, Inc.
Library Consultant: Kathleen Baxter

Art Director: LuAnn Ascheman-Adams
Creative Director: Joe Ewest
Editorial Director: Nick Healy
Managing Editor: Catherine Neitge

Library of Congress Cataloging-in-Publication Data
Donovan, Sandra, 1967–
   Teens in Thailand / by Sandy Donovan.
      p. cm. — (Global Connections)
   Includes index.
   ISBN 978-0-7565-4046-3 (library binding)
   1. Teenagers—Thailand—Social conditions—Juvenile literature.
   2. Teenagers—Thailand—Social life and customs—Juvenile literature.
   3. Thailand—Social conditions—21st century—Juvenile literature.
   4. Thailand–Social life and customs—21st century—Juvenile literature. I. Title.
   HQ799.T5D66 2009
   305.23509593—dc22   2008035714

Visit Compass Point Books on the Internet at www.compasspointbooks.com
or e-mail your request to custserv@compasspointbooks.com

Table of Contents

Bangkok

INDIAN OCEAN

MONGOLIA

SOUTH KOREA

PACIFIC
OCEAN

CHINA

BHUTAN

BANGLADESH

MYANMAR

LAOS

VIETNAM

PHILIPPINES

THAILAND

KAMPUCHEA

BRUNEI

MALAYSIA

MALAYSIA

SINGAPORE

INDONESIA

TEENS IN THAILAND

A VARIETY OF ACTIVITIES KEEPS TEENS BUSY IN THE SOUTHEAST ASIAN NATION OF THAILAND. Thai teens might attend early morning ceremonies at ancient Buddhist temples. On weekend afternoons, they may be found hanging out at a shopping mall—or plowing a rice paddy. Their evenings are sometimes spent in downtown dance clubs—or at a rural farming festival. As citizens of a more than 700-year-old nation, they grow up with a strong sense of their own culture. From this culture, they learn a sense of community and respect for elders, but they also live in a time of rapid development. A fast-changing economy and new technology impact their lives greatly.

Today teens ages 15 to 19 make up about 9 percent of Thailand's total population. There is no "typical" Thai teen. Some live in the fast-paced world of Thailand's modern capital, Bangkok. Others live in the slower world of Thailand's rural villages. Most Thai teens find a way to balance their culture with the influences of the modern world as they go to school, hang out with friends and family, and look forward to the future.

There are seven levels to the education system in Thailand: kindergarten, primary, secondary, pre-university, higher, special, and adult education.

1

School Days

THE DAY IS BEGINNING AT A HIGH SCHOOL IN DOWNTOWN BANGKOK. It's just after 7:30 A.M., and the halls are crowded with students. School usually starts at 8:30. However, students have to arrive before 7:50 or they will be marked late. Most schools raise the Thai flag and play the national anthem at 8 A.M. The halls are a sea of navy and white uniforms—light shirts and navy skirts or shorts—as the students make their way to their homerooms. Inside the classrooms, desks are neatly arranged in rows. At the front of each room is a picture of Thailand's King Bhumibol Adulyadej, along with an image of Buddha, the symbol of Buddhism, Thailand's national religion. Thailand's red, white, and blue flag also hangs at the front of the room.

About 40 students take their places in each classroom. In homeroom, the students hear announcements for the day. Sometimes they hear reminders about school rules. At most high schools, students are assigned duties for the week during homeroom, including cleaning the bathroom, the hallways, or

School Lunch

In rural Thailand, many children return home from school in the middle of the day to share a meal with their families. If school is far from home, students bring a midday meal with them and eat at school. In urban Thailand, almost all students eat lunch at school. Schools have cafeterias where students can either buy lunch or eat something they brought from home. In public schools, the government keeps lunch prices low.

For most students, it is cheaper to buy lunch than to bring it from home. A typical hot lunch of chicken fried in chili paste served with fried egg and rice might cost about 15 baht (U.S. 44 cents). Drinks usually cost about 3 baht (U.S. 9 cents). In larger schools, students can often choose from three or four different meals each day.

the cafeteria. At 8:25, they leave their homerooms for their first class, which lasts 50 minutes. Five or six more class periods will follow, as well as time for lunch in the school cafeteria.

Modern Thai high schools, commonly found in larger cities, can have more than 1,000 students between the ages of 13 and 18. Typically a high school has six four-story buildings made of concrete and glass, with classrooms, computer labs, science labs, and art studios inside.

Schools in rural Thailand are quite different. Often several small villages share one high school, which may be a one- or two-room building made of wood. There are no computer or science labs and perhaps only 50 students in the entire school.

Even though the schools are distinctive, both urban and rural Thailand share the same dedication to learning. More than 90 percent of Thai adults (91 percent of women and 95 percent of men) can read and write.

Commitment to Education

For many Thais, education begins in preschool and ends 20 years later with a university degree. Nine years of school—from about ages 7 to 16—are required by law. The government provides free public education for students until they reach grade 9. Almost all schools are co-ed—boys and girls attend the same schools. Students go to school each year from mid-May

School uniforms can cost around 400 to 600 baht (U.S.$11.80 to $17.65) each. Families who cannot afford the uniform cannot send their children to school.

until the end of March. This gives Thai students a vacation during April, the country's hottest month.

Almost all Thai children attend primary school. However, not all schools are equal. Some of the more prestigious primary schools require students to pass an entrance exam before being admitted. Graduates of these selective schools are more likely to attend a university later in life.

Primary school includes grades one through six. Students learn subjects such as math, science, reading, and writing in Thai, the country's national language. Beginning in first grade, all Thai students are also required to study the English language. English classes focus mostly on learning vocabulary and grammar. As a result, many Thai students can write some English but not speak it.

More than 95 percent of all students finish the sixth grade. At the end of sixth grade, students take an exam. When they pass, they receive a certificate of completion and move on to secondary school.

Students can attend either private or public secondary schools. Public schools are free, while private schools charge a yearly fee. Both kinds of schools have entrance exams. Secondary school is divided into two parts: lower secondary and upper secondary. Lower secondary, grades seven through nine, is called *mathayom* 1 to mathayom 3. Upper secondary includes grades 10 through 12, or mathayom 4 to mathayom 6. Often lower and upper secondary schools are located in the same building.

In lower secondary school, students study Thai, science, math, social studies, art, career education, and health and physical education. They also learn English and other foreign languages, including Japanese and Arabic.

Eighty percent of all students com-

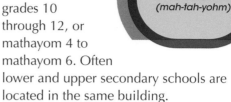

mathayom
(mah-tah-yohm)

Some private schools include religious education as a part of their programs.

plete grade nine, earning a certificate of lower secondary education. To get into upper secondary school, they must take another exam.

Upper secondary schools are divided into two tracks: academic and vocational. Some high schools offer only one or the other. Others, called comprehensive schools, offer both programs.

The academic track prepares students who are planning to attend a university. These students study Thai, social studies, physical education, science, mathematics, foreign languages, and arts and crafts.

The vocational track prepares students for the working world. Some vocational students want to get a job right after high school, while others plan to go to a technical college. Others want to attend a university but did not do well enough on the entrance exam to get into the academic track.

Lower Secondary School Schedule

Monday	Tuesday	Wednesday	Thursday	Friday
art	P.E.	math	Thai	science
geography	math	math (optional)	English	
math	Buddhism		geography	Thai
lunch	lunch	lunch	lunch	lunch
Thai	science	electronics	math	economics
English	career guidance		P.E.	English
science (optional)	English	hygiene	economics	Buddhism
	Thai	Scouts	club	math

Vocational students take classes in Thai, social studies, physical education, and science. For the rest of their classes, they choose one of five fields: technology, business education, arts and crafts, agriculture, or home economics. Many vocational high schools also offer a one-year trade program; upon completion, students receive a tradesman certificate. Any student who finishes lower secondary school can choose this option. With the tradesman certificate, a student is

Scouting

The Scout Promise says: *On my honour I promise that I will be loyal to the Nation, the Religion, and the King; help other people at all times; and obey the Scout Law.*

Scouting has been a major part of Thai life since King Rama VI first introduced it in 1911. Today King Bhumibol is the country's chief scout, the head of the country's Scout Association. Just about every teen in Thailand has been a member of the National Scout Organization of Thailand. Being a scout is mandatory at most schools. Both boys and girls can be scouts—a Cub Scout (ages 8 to 11), Scout (ages 11 to 16), Senior Scout (ages 14 to 18), or Rover (ages 16 to 25). Most schools have meetings once a week. On that day students wear their khaki scout uniforms to school.

The scouts reflect the Thai values of respect and helping others. Thailand's scouting motto states, "It's better to die than to lie." Scout troops participate in community service and often help out in floods and fires, and with first aid.

In 2003, Thailand hosted the 20th World Scout Jamboree. More than 30,000 scouts from all over the globe participated.

Teen Scenes

In a modern apartment on the outskirts of Bangkok, a 15-year-old boy wakes up to his blaring alarm clock. It's 6 A.M. The clock is playing a song by one of his favorite Japanese bands. He quickly switches it off and rubs his eyes. Although he thinks about falling back to sleep, he knows he needs to be at school on time. Plus, he hears his mother cooking him breakfast. He hops out of bed and gets dressed—school uniforms make it easy to choose an outfit. He grabs his backpack and goes to the kitchen. He's happy to see that his mom has made his favorite breakfast, *Khao Man Kai*, or stewed chicken with rice. Unfortunately, he has to eat it fast because it's time to meet his friends to go to school. They have to walk several blocks, catch a city bus, and then transfer to a smaller pickup truck used for public transportation.

Khao Man kai
(cow-muhn-kah)

Nearly 400 miles (640 kilometers) to the north, another 15-year-old boy wakes up at the same time. Instead of using an alarm clock, he gets up with the sun. He slept all night in a hammock in the same room as his parents and two sisters. They all wake up at the same time. His sisters will help his mother begin cooking breakfast while he goes with his father to get fresh water. Their one-room wooden house sits high on stilts. He and his father climb down a ladder with the water buckets. Underneath the house are pigs and chickens that the family raises for food. After breakfast the boy will feed the animals and do some other chores before beginning the nearly two-mile (three-km) walk to school. At age 14, the boy wanted to drop out of school to help his father with farm work, but his parents insisted he continue his education. Neither of his parents finished high school, so the boy's own graduation is important.

These two Thai teens live quite different lives, but they have much in common. They both respect their families and other elders in their lives. They both have parents who value education and make sure they get to school every day. They are two different but typical Thai teens.

17

qualified to get a job without finishing all three years of upper secondary school.

Across Thailand, nearly 80 percent of teenagers complete grade 12 and graduate from secondary school. Most of the students who do not graduate are from low-income families. They often drop out because they are needed at home or because they need to earn money to help support their families. Other times, they drop out because it is too difficult to get to school or the fees are too high. (Beginning in grade 10, students pay fees to attend school.) In the past, there were few secondary schools in rural Thailand. However, in recent years, the government has established more secondary schools and other programs to help needy families.

On to College

Thailand has 780 public (government-funded) and private schools offering post-high school education. Getting into the best colleges and universities is not easy, though. In the late 1990s, only about 26 percent of young Thais received higher education. Until that time, Thai families needed to earn a relatively high income to afford to send their teenagers to college. In the late 1990s, the Thai government started offering low-interest loans to help pay for higher education. This assistance helped more families afford college or a university. Today more and more high school graduates are going on to college. Still, getting accepted remains difficult.

After graduating from upper secondary school, students take an intensive exam to be admitted to a public university. The exam, called the Joint Higher Education Entrance Examination (JHEEE), is offered once each year, in April. Thai teens spend up to two years studying for it. In fact, many students start worrying about the JHEEE while they are still in primary school.

The JHEEE is divided into various subjects. Students take different sections

Teacher's Day (Wan Waikhru)

On January 16, students throughout Thailand recognize the importance of their teachers. Many teens find a simple way to pay respect to their teachers, bowing before them and bringing flowers. Some families visit a temple to make merit, or give offerings, in the name of all teachers.

College students are expected to do between 15 and 18 hours of coursework a week.

of the test depending on where they are applying. Universities are divided into programs of studies called faculties. Students can apply to up to five faculties at one or more universities. Only about 30 percent of students who take the test are accepted to a university. Students have to take an exam to be admitted to private schools as well. Getting into a private college or university is just as hard as being admitted to a university. Once students are accepted to college— public or private—they prepare themselves for several years of hard work. Most students earn bachelor's degrees in four years. It takes five years to earn a bachelor's degree in pharmaceuticals or graphic arts. Students take two

additional years to become a doctor of medicine, doctor of dental surgery, or doctor of veterinary medicine.

It is easier to get accepted into technical schools, where students can prepare for jobs in business admin- istration, manufacturing, and other industries. Students who go to a technical college can earn a diploma in vocational or technical education in two years. Diplomas are awarded in agriculture, arts and crafts, trade and industry, or business. Students who earn these degrees can either go on to get a job or apply to a four-year college or university.

Students catch rides on songthaeos, trucks that travel throughout the city. The backs are open to allow passengers easy entrances and exits.

2 At Home in the City or Country

IT'S 4 P.M. IN BANGKOK, AND MOST OF THE CITY'S SCHOOLS ARE OUT FOR THE DAY. Many students stay after school for clubs, sports, and activities. Chess club, scouting groups, English-language conversation clubs, and soccer teams are all popular after-school activities for Thai teens. Lots of other students head home right after their last class.

In a city known for its traffic jams, traveling to and from school can be a major headache. On many roads in Bangkok, traffic moves less than 5 miles (8 km) per hour for most of the day. Teens who live close enough avoid the rush by walking to and from school, but they have to be careful. Despite the slow-moving traffic, crossing Bangkok's streets can be dangerous. It's often hard for pedestrians to see fast-zooming motorcycles as the bikes attempt to weave through traffic.

Teens who live farther from school often rely on a variety of public transportation. Full-sized city buses and smaller buses called songthaeos serve the metro area.

songthaeos
(song-tows)

21

Bangkok's Legendary Traffic

Bangkok traffic jams have been called some of the worst in the world. It's not uncommon for traffic on Bangkok streets to be at a standstill for long periods of time. People are used to allowing hours for a commute that would take 15 minutes if traffic were moving.

The city's explosive growth during the 1980s and 1990s is part of the reason traffic is so bad in Bangkok. The city doesn't have enough roads to accommodate all the cars, which have become a status symbol in Thailand. Even though it might be faster to take a bus, many Thais will travel only in their own cars.

The city has tried to deal with its traffic problems by introducing mass transit systems. In 1999, the elevated SkyTrain opened to the public, allowing passengers to travel for only 15 to 40 baht (U.S. 44 cents to $1.20) per trip. Yet the SkyTrain only reaches limited parts of the city. Many Bangkok residents have never ridden on it.

In 2004, the government opened an underground train system called the Mass Rapid Transit (MRT). It cost the country more than 93 billion baht (U.S.$2.75 billion) and seven years to complete. At some stops, it connects with the SkyTrain, allowing passengers to transfer between train systems. Ticket prices are similar to those of the SkyTrain. City planners hoped that 400,000 people a day would ride it, but because of its limited range only about 150,000 do.

For now, many Bangkok residents just put up with the traffic. It will be up to today's teenagers to solve the problem in the future.

In Thai, songthaeo means "two rows," a suitable name for pickup trucks fitted with two rows of covered seats in the truck bed area. Smaller three-wheeled vehicles called *tuk-tuks* offer cheap rides throughout Thailand. An elevated train and an underground metro system also weave through downtown Bangkok. Frequent stops and traffic delays slow down all of these

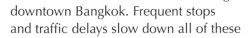

tuk-tuks
(dtook-dtook)

transportation methods in Thailand's capital city. It can take urban teens a couple of hours to get to and from school each day.

Life in the City

Dealing with traffic jams is just one of the ways that life for urban Thai teenagers is different from life for rural teens. About one-third of Thailand's 65 million residents live in a city. Of those, more than half live in or around Bangkok, which has almost 10 million residents. The next largest Thai city is Chiang Mai,

Chiang Mai has been called Thailand's "second capital."

23

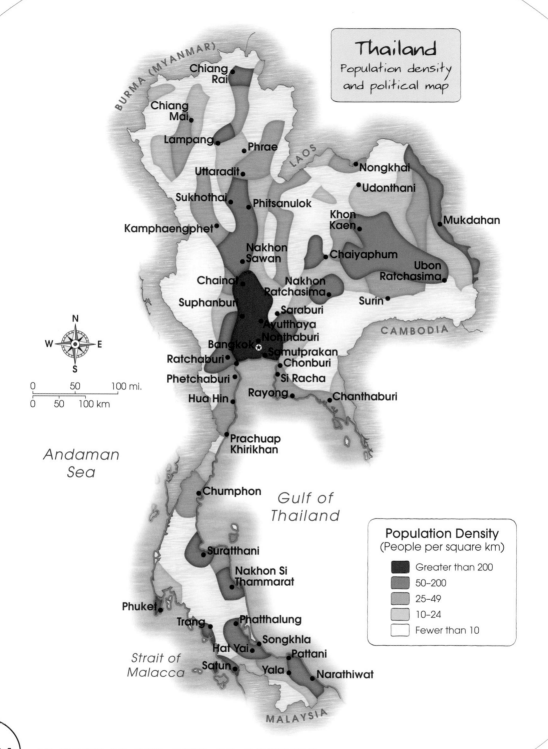

Thailand
Population density
and political map

BURMA (MYANMAR)

Chiang
Rai

Chiang
Mai

Lampang

Phrae

LAOS

Uttaradit

Nongkhai

Udonthani

Sukhothai

Phitsanulok

Khon
Kaen

Mukdahan

Kamphaengphet

Nakhon
Sawan

Chaiyaphum

Ubon
Ratchasima

Chainat

Nakhon
Ratchasima

Suphanburi

Surin

Saraburi

Ayutthaya

CAMBODIA

Bangkok

Nonthaburi

Samutprakan

Ratchaburi

Chonburi

Phetchaburi

Si Racha

Hua Hin

Rayong

Chanthaburi

Andaman
Sea

Prachuap
Khirikhan

N
W   E
S

0   50   100 mi.

0   50   100 km

Chumphon

Gulf of
Thailand

Suratthani

Nakhon Si
Thammarat

Population Density
(People per square km)

Greater than 200

50–200

25–49

10–24

Fewer than 10

Phuket

Trang

Phatthalung

Songkhla

Hat Yai

Pattani

Strait of
Malacca

Satun

Yala

Narathiwat

MALAYSIA

which has fewer than 300,000 residents.

Urban Thai teens in middle- and upper-income families live with many modern conveniences. Most have their own bedrooms in large houses or apartments. In the late 1980s and early 1990s, the Thai economy boomed, and many modern condominiums went up around Bangkok. The buildings are often towering glass structures with doormen to greet and watch out for residents. They might have a swimming pool or health club, and services such as grocery stores and hair salons on the ground floor. Individual apartments feature spacious rooms, marble baths, and sometimes floor-to-ceiling windows and balconies overlooking the city.

In the late 1990s, the economy suffered, but the fancy condominiums remained. Today upper-income Thai families still call these residences home.

There are more than 27 million cell phone users throughout Thailand. MP3 players are also popular accessories.

Apartments, townhomes, houses, and condos are spread across Bangkok.

Teens in these families are likely to have stereos in their bedrooms, as well as televisions, cell phones, video games, computers, and personal music players that they use all day.

Urban teens from middle-income families have many of the same luxuries. However, they live in more modest apartment buildings or traditional, two-story Thai houses made of teakwood. The first story of the house is usually a family business, while the second story is used for living space. Often teens share a bedroom with a sibling. Since teakwood has become too expensive for most people to afford, newer houses, often located in the suburbs of Bangkok, are made of concrete and brick. All traditional houses feature many balconies and other openings to the outside.

Urban Thai teens usually make their trip home from school with friends, perhaps stopping for a snack along the way. They might purchase snacks at one of the food stalls that sell traditional Thai food or at a modern fast-food restaurant. Western restaurants such as McDonalds, Pizza Hut, KFC, and Burger King can all be found in Bangkok.

Barely Getting By

Urban teens from lower-income families live quite different lives. Many low-income families earn their money selling food at roadside stands, working as unskilled construction workers, or finding other service work on a daily basis. Because they don't earn enough

Inflation is one of the main reasons the number of poor and homeless people in Thailand has increased. In 2008, the government handed out coupons to help families buy necessities.

money to pay for suitable places to live, they often live in ramshackle housing projects called shantytowns. Many of these houses were built quickly out of any available building materials, such as wood or tin. Other houses, made of concrete, were built and paid for by the government.

Most of these houses do not have electricity to run lights, fans, or air conditioners. Some don't even have windows. With an average temperature of 77 to 95 degrees Fahrenheit (25 to 35 degrees Celsius), sleeping may be difficult. Poor-quality housing is often located in the swampiest areas of the city. With a five-month rainy season—from June to October—many of these homes flood often.

Wave of Devastation

A national disaster devastated Thailand on December 26, 2004, when a giant tsunami swept across the Indian Ocean. The huge tidal wave wiped out more than 250 miles (400 km) of Thailand's coastline. In Thailand alone, 9,000 people died and 1,200 children were orphaned. Thousands more were affected by the event. More than 35,000 families lost their work and means of supporting their families. Another 50,000 children were impacted because at least 200 schools lost teachers, students, or buildings. In total, more than 200,000 people across the Indian Ocean lost their lives.

The 2004 disaster is labeled as the worst tsunami and one of the top 10 earthquakes on record. Today residents in Thailand, Indonesia, Malaysia, India, and other nearby countries continue to rebuild from this tragedy. The United Nations estimates that it will be the costliest disaster ever recorded, taking some areas up to a decade to financially recover. In 2005, the Thai government spent nearly 34 billion baht (U.S.$1 billion) in aid.

More than 400 fishing villages were wiped out by the tsunami.

Life in the Country

Living conditions for rural teens stand in stark contrast to what their urban peers have. About two-thirds of the population live in rural areas. Most are concentrated in the central plain area, a fertile region best suited for farming. There Thailand's most important river, the Chao Phraya, keeps the soil moist. Families in this region are mostly rice farmers. Along the eastern coast, many families make a living picking fruit, growing rubber, or catching fish in the South China Sea.

Farming and fishing families in central Thailand usually live in traditional Thai houses. These wooden houses are built on poles, which keep the living spaces off of the ground and out of danger from floods and crawling animals. However, living high off the ground doesn't keep out the mosquitoes. In Thailand's hot, humid climate, mosquitoes can be a problem. Houses are often built with many openings to catch as much breeze as possible, making it easy for mosquitoes to come in. Since mosquitoes are attracted to standing water, Thai families are careful not to leave buckets or bowls of water around. In houses with no running water, this can make life quite difficult.

The northeastern area of Thailand, called Isan, is the poorest region of the

Stilt houses can be made from many materials, including sheet metal, wood, and bamboo.

country. Many people there are rice farmers, but since the area doesn't get as much rain as central Thailand, the rice crop is not as good. Teens here are less likely to finish high school and often have to work in the rice fields during the growing season. During the off-season, entire families move frequently in order to find work. Some go to Bangkok to work as unskilled construction workers. Teens from Isan commonly leave home in their early teens and move to Bangkok to try to earn money.

In Thailand's cool, northern mountainous region lies the country's highest mountain, Doi Inthanon. It towers 8,500 feet (2,576 meters) above sea level. Families in this region also live in traditional Thai houses, but with temperatures reaching as low as 50 F (10 C), they don't need to worry about mosquitoes as much as their southern neighbors. People in northern Thailand often work as farmers, operating pig and poultry farms and growing tropical fruits such as lychees, longans, pineapples, and oranges. World-famous Thai silk, one of the finest fabrics in the world,

Making traditional crafts and tools to sell to tourists is one way people earn money.

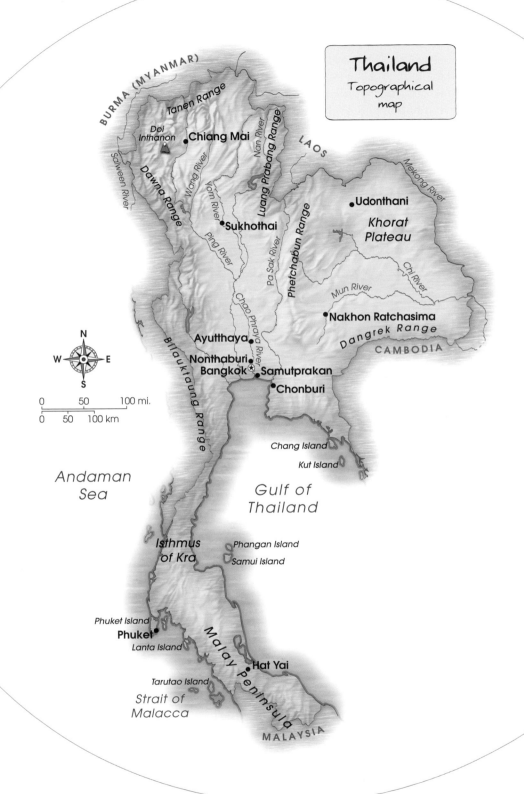

Thailand
Topographical
map

BURMA (MYANMAR)

Tanen Range

Doi
Inthanon
● Chiang Mai

Nan River

Luang Prabang Range

LAOS

Mekong River

Salween River

Dawna Range

Wang River

Yom River

Ping River

● Sukhothai

Pa Sak River

Phetchabun Range

● Udonthani

Khorat
Plateau

Chi River

Mun River

● Nakhon Ratchasima

Dangrek Range

CAMBODIA

Chao Phraya River

Ayutthaya ●
Nonthaburi ●
Bangkok ● ● Samutprakan
● Chonburi

N
W   E
S

0   50   100 mi.
0   50   100 km

Bilauktaung Range

Chang Island

Kut Island

Andaman
Sea

Gulf of
Thailand

Isthmus
of Kra

Phangan Island

Samui Island

Phuket Island
● Phuket

Lanta Island

Malay Peninsula

● Hat Yai

Tarutao Island

Strait of
Malacca

MALAYSIA

comes from this area where some people make a living raising silkworms. Many people also still make traditional Thai handicrafts such as pottery and woodcarving. Because the northern region is a popular vacation spot, some families make their living by serving tourists.

Thailand's southern region, a peninsula that runs between the Gulf of Thailand and the Andaman Sea, has some of the world's most beautiful white-sand beaches. Inland, the peninsula is a rain forest with many varieties of tropical animals. The beaches are popular vacation spots for middle- and upper-income teens and their families. International travelers also frequent Thailand's beautiful southern coast.

Most teens living in Thailand's rural areas have fewer modern conveniences than urban Thai teens. Most don't have computers, cell phones, or MP3 players and have never been to a McDonald's or Pizza Hut. Although most rural families have at least one car and sometimes a motorcycle, vehicles are used mainly to haul farm equipment, not for transportation. Instead of taking a bus or driving to school, teens frequently ride a bicycle. Sometimes they catch a ride on someone's truck if their school is a long way from home.

Teens in the central plains area might have radios or televisions, but such devices are often useless in most of northeastern Thailand where few people have electricity. Recently the Thai government began a project to bring solar-generated electricity to some of the country's more remote areas. Part of the project's goal is to teach Thais how to set up and maintain solar power stations. This kind of technical knowledge will help them change their future.

Noodle bowls, soups, grilled meat, sausages, dumplings, and fried foods are commonly found along Thailand's busy streets.

Sharing Meals

Wherever Thai teens live, mealtime is an important part of their day. For centuries, meals in Thailand have represented the Thai values of beauty, balance, sharing, and respect. Thai dishes usually contain meat or fish cooked with vegetables and spices such as garlic and ginger. Steamed white rice is almost always served on the side, along with elaborately carved fruits and vegetables. Thai chefs try to balance the flavors of each dish among four main tastes: sweet, salty, spicy, and sour. Fresh herbs (rather than dried) are also heavily used. Besides ginger and garlic, other

nam pla
(nahm-plah)

common condiments are lemongrass, lime juice, and a salty fish sauce known as *nam pla*.

At mealtime, each dish is shared among everyone at the table. Even at a restaurant, Thais do not order a main course for themselves. Instead, they order several dishes—usually one per

Pizza Hut Thailand has added several pizza toppings to appeal to its Asian customers. Original toppings include corn, capsicum, prawns, and squid.

person—and share them all. The main dishes, along with bowls of rice, are placed in the center of the table. People try each dish by placing one spoonful at a time on their individual plate. It's considered rude to put more than one spoonful at a time on one's plate. For eating utensils, Thais traditionally use chopsticks—a custom brought to Thailand from nearby China—or simply a fork and spoon.

In fact, the country's Southeast Asian neighbors have influenced most of Thailand's cuisine. The Chinese shared many cooking styles with Thailand, such as fast-cooking meats and vegetables in a stir-fry. Chinese also brought noodles to Thailand, and today, one of the most popular Thai dishes around the world is phat Thai, or stir-fried noodles. Thai chefs have borrowed spices from other neighbors, including Vietnam, Cambodia, and Indonesia. The spice curry came from India, but Thais added their own twists. While Indian curries are usually yellow, spicy Thai curries are most often green or red (the difference is the type of peppers used to make the curry as well as the amount of turmeric added).

International fare from places such as Italy, France, Japan, and India are becoming more common. The chefs will often add their own preparations to the more traditional preparations, creating their own fusion cuisine. Iced coffee, cappuccino, and espresso are also making an appearance, popping up at restaurants, bakeries, coffee bars, and even gas stations.

When to Eat?

Today many Thai teens and their families are too busy to sit down together for traditional lunches and dinners. Most students eat lunch at their school cafeteria. After school, they may stop at a fast-food restaurant, but they probably won't grab a hamburger. Fast-food restaurants in Thailand have adapted their menus to Thai tastes. Since Thais eat very little ground beef, McDonald's restaurants in Thailand offer more chicken and fish sandwiches and fewer hamburgers than McDonald's in other parts of the world. One teen wrote:

Lots of teenagers in Thailand like to eat at a fast food restaurant because now it has become fashionable. … When Thai boys go out with their girlfriend, they always go to [a] fast food restaurant because it is expensive and she will be impress[ed].

When they do sit down to eat a meal together, Thai families often eat traditional food. For dinner a family will often share dishes of stir-fried meat, fish, and vegetables—but they may do so in front of the television. Instead of chopsticks they may use a fork and spoon. Knives are rarely used at the table because most Thai food is cut into bite-size pieces before cooking.

The population in Thailand is getting older. There were 1.2 million elderly people in 1960—this number increased to more than 4 million in 1990, and is expected to reach nearly 11 million by 2020.

3

Family Influence

NO MATTER HOW MUCH THE COUNTRY HAS CHANGED, FAMILY IS STILL THE CENTER OF THAI LIFE.

Traditionally families included an average of six children, but in the past few decades, smaller families have become much more common. Today the typical family includes just two children.

About 60 percent of all families are nuclear—children live with their parents. However, most Thai teens have a close relationship with their extended family and live with their grandparents for at least part of their lives. A typical family might start out as a nuclear family. When a daughter marries, her husband moves in with her family. Newlyweds often live with the wife's parents until their first child is born, when the couple moves into their own house. Then they are a nuclear family again. Still, they will remain close with both the wife's and the husband's parents. When grandparents grow old enough to need help, they will often move in with their children.

Respect for Elders

Respecting elders is central to Thai culture, and Thai children understand this from a young age. It means that they listen to older relatives and family friends as well as their own parents. As they grow up, they are likely to consider how their grandparents would react to their behavior choices.

Gratitude is an important part of the respect that Thai youth have for their elders. One of the worst insults is to tell people that they are ungrateful to their elders. Thai children and teens often thank their parents for the time and money they have spent taking care of them. In return for their parents' generosity, teens expect to take care of their parents later in life. There are hardly any nursing homes in Thailand—most Thais would find the idea of sending elders to live by themselves absurd. There are also few formal retirement plans or pensions to provide income to retired people. Traditionally, grown children took care of their parents by having them live with them. This was simple when extended families usually lived in the same area. Today it's more common for family members to move to other parts of Thailand. Most often, young people will move from a rural area to a city where job prospects are better. In these cases, the younger generation sends money home to elderly parents and relatives.

The Thai language has several unique words that express the value the culture places on older people. For instance, children call their siblings by different names, depending on whether

New Nicknames

Family names, or surnames, are a relatively modern phenomenon in Thailand. In fact, in the past, people were usually known by their first names only. When the use of surnames became more popular, Chinese immigrants changed their surnames in order to sound more Thai.

Thais know the meaning of their names, which are usually taken from Pali or Sanskrit words. Parents try to give children names that reflect something good, such as Chaichana (Champion) or Piyathida (Dear Daughter).

One-syllable nicknames are common for day-to-day use. The latest trend is to use English-language words as nicknames. In fact, one survey found that more than half of elementary school students have English nicknames, while 40 percent of high school students and 6 percent of university students do. The most popular names often have to do with pop culture or money. Some of the trendiest English nicknames include Oil, Bank, Tomcruise, Elizabeth, Army, Kiwi, Charlie, and even God.

Teen pregnancies and higher numbers of children living away from their parents, along with smaller family size, are all credited to the fraying family bonds in Thailand.

they are older or younger. They also call their aunts and uncles by different titles, depending on whether the aunts and uncles are older or younger than the child's parents.

Thais also use these names for people they meet on the streets—whether they know them or not. For instance, a person of any age would address a waitress as "older sister" or "younger sister," depending on the waitress's age.

Family Terms

Relative	Name
Grandmother: mother's mother	Yai (yuy)
Grandfather: mother's father	Ta (tah)
Grandmother: father's mother	Ya (yah)
Grandfather: father's father	Pu (poo)
Aunt or Uncle: older sibling of father	Lung (lung)
Aunt or Uncle: older sibling of mother	Pa (pah)
Aunt or Uncle: younger sibling of mother	Na (nah)
Aunt or Uncle: younger sibling of father	Ah (ah)

Modern Ways

Life in Thailand is changing quickly. Today modern ideas are competing with traditional Thai values. Thai teens are influenced by many different cultures. In particular, teens living in cities are exposed to a variety of new ideas and values that come mostly from Japan, Western Europe, and North America.

Dress and fashion trends are one of the most obvious signs of Thailand's changing culture. Traditional Thai dress is most often a loose-fitting cotton shirt and pants for males, and a long, slim cotton skirt for women. In many rural areas, most people still wear traditional dress. But in cities, it is more common to see clothing with a Western or Japanese influence. Teens especially embrace the latest fashion trends from Japan, Europe, and the United States. These fashions include jeans and T-shirts for boys as well as shorter skirts, more revealing tops, and tighter pants for girls. Today it is just as common to see a teenager dressed in trendy styles in downtown Bangkok as it is in Tokyo, London, or New York. A marketing consultant in Bangkok observed:

Thailand is very receptive to outside cultures, very forward looking—a lot of what they do locally and culturally

Hair, clothing, nails, braces, and cell phones are only some of the ways Thai teens show off their style sense.

comes from other places. Many trends start with music. When you embrace music, you start to explore how that music is represented—the style and the look. It then gets followed by fashion, followed by lifestyle, mentality, and outlook.

However, not everyone from the older generation approves of the latest styles and trends. Even the schools and government have gotten involved in this fashion debate. In 1998, Chulalongkorn University, one of the country's largest colleges, banned miniskirts. In 2007, a famous Thai actress known as Chotiros got in trouble at Thammasat University where she was a student. The school said she had worn an indecent dress to the Subhanahongsa Awards, Thailand's version of the Oscars. As a result,

Chotiros had to perform community service at her university.

Thai teens take fashion beyond clothes. For many years, Thai teens have copied the Japanese fad of carrying their cell phones by giant, brightly colored straps. Decorative cases and custom downloads such as ring tones, wallpaper, and games have also been immensely popular. Today teens in Bangkok are following the Japanese fascination with *dekoden*. Dekoden, which means "phone decoration" in Japanese, is the art of decorating the

dekoden
(deh-koh-dehn)

Supplies for dekoden can be found at markets, gift shops, stationery stores, and even nail salons.

Evolution of Dating

The art of dating has come alive in today's Thailand. Until very recently, most marriages were arranged, with parents or grandparents choosing a suitable partner for their sons or daughters. In some cases, teenagers chose their own partners, but they always asked for their parents' permission before marrying. If their parents disagreed with the marriage, most young people would honor that decision.

Public affection—even holding hands—was never displayed. Living together as a couple before marriage was absolutely unheard of. Today the whole concept of dating and relationships is evolving—particularly in the cities. Most Thai teens today choose girlfriends or boyfriends when they are as young as 13 or 14 years old.

There has been a recent change in the way Thai teens see themselves and their romantic lives. It has been estimated that there are more than 10,000 transgendered people living throughout the country—one of the largest populations in the world.

Although many elder Thais disapprove, public displays of affection are becoming more common, and some Thai couples live together and have children before they get married.

43

actual phone itself. Street stalls through-out downtown Bangkok offer to paint, apply decals, and even embed fake diamonds and beads into cell phones. With close to 41 million cell phone users in Thailand, you don't have to look far to see dekoden in practice.

Cell phone decorations range in price, depending on the design and intricacy. Less expensive items, such as 3-D stickers and fake gems, can cost around 200 baht (U.S.$6), while more expensive items, such as Swarovski crystals, airbrushed designs, and more complex beading and design can cost up to 3,000 baht (U.S.$90).

Stuck On You

Another Thai fashion craze involves decorating teeth. Across Thailand, but mostly in Bangkok, teens are jumping on this trend. Teeth decoration starts with braces. Instead of trying to make braces look as inconspicuous as possible, Thai teens do whatever they can to make their braces stand out, wearing bright red, yellow, and green rubber bands on them. Brightly colored braces became such a fashion statement that even those who didn't need—or couldn't afford—real braces wanted them.

Stores began selling do-it-yourself

Weakening Ties?

Although family ties remain important in Thailand, the bonds may be loosening. In the past, Thai children grew up living with or very near their parents and extended family. Today increased migration from rural to urban areas is changing that. One study found that grandparents were raising more than 37 percent of children living in rural Thailand because their parents had moved to a city. Even when children move with their parents to a city, they may spend less time with them. Another survey found that 43 percent of parents felt distant from their children because they only spent between one to three hours a day with them.

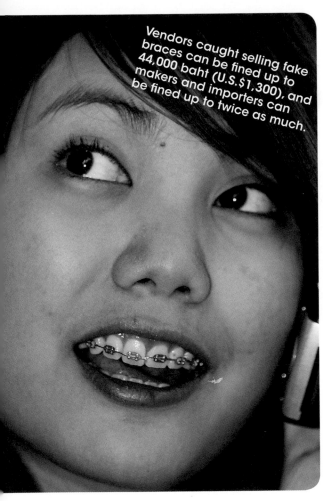

Vendors caught selling fake braces can be fined up to 44,000 baht (U.S.$1,300), and makers and importers can be fined up to twice as much.

In 2006, the government passed a law against selling fake braces. Teens who wear the braces don't get into trouble, but adults who sell them can be fined or sent to prison. Since the law was passed, the craze of decorating teeth has slowed down but not disappeared entirely.

A Place To Live

Living arrangements are another expression of changing culture. In the past, Thai teens and young adults almost always lived with their parents until or even after marriage. Today it is more common for young adults to rent their own apartments in Bangkok and other Thai cities. Teens often move out of their parents' house to attend a university and do not move back. In their 20s, as they get their first jobs, they live with roommates or partners in urban apartments. However, they are still likely to stay in close touch with their families. Many teens begin to support their parents or grandparents while they are still quite young.

Today Thai teens balance the traditions of their older relatives and the influences of modern life. Teens—especially urban teens—dress and act quite differently from their parents or grandparents at their age. Even as they embrace modern culture, they remain close to their families. Showing respect and gratitude to elders continues to be a key Thai value.

kits, which allowed teens to apply fake braces that they could decorate however they wanted. Many adults were worried about the health issues of wearing fake braces that could cut the inside of a person's mouth and lead to an infection. Or they were concerned they could come loose and choke the wearer.

Many holidays in Thailand have Buddhist origins. The country even uses Buddhist era dates for some holidays—when the rest of the world celebrates the year 2010, Thais will be celebrating 2553.

4 Celebrating Religion and Nation

OUTSIDE A MODERN-STYLE HOUSE IN THE BANGKOK SUBURBS IS A SCENE THAT LOOKS AS IF IT COULD HAVE TAKEN PLACE SEVERAL CENTURIES EARLIER. Along both sides of the street stand children, teens, and adults dressed in formal, traditional Thai clothes. Each person has a partner on the other side of the street, and each of these pairs holds a brightly colored silk ribbon across the pathway. Music is playing in the distance. Soon a small parade of people appears. It's a groom's procession. They are making their way to the bride's parents' house in a traditional Thai wedding-day procession.

The groom's group includes several people holding arches made of banana leaves and palm tree branches. Under the arches, the groom walks with his "bearers"— young men and women carrying wedding gifts and the dowry. The group stops as it approaches each pair holding the silk ribbons. To pass through each silk "gate," the groom has to pay a small toll.

As the music plays on, he hands each pair some coins or a small gift. Soon he has passed through each gate and arrives at his bride's front door. But before he can enter, he has one last "gate" to pass through. At the doorway stands the bride's grandfather or another respected elder. The groom offers him a larger gift. Finally, the groom enters the house. There he finds the bride and the rest of her relatives.

The last to arrive at the wedding ceremony are the Buddhist monks. These religious figures perform the actual ceremony. Monks—almost always nine of them—arrive at the wedding and seat themselves in a semicircle around the guests. Then

While traditional weddings are still common, Western influences have changed what brides and grooms wear on their special day.

the bride and groom light a candle, and the ceremony begins. First the monks chant. Then the bride and groom offer food to the monks. This Buddhist tradition is called "making merit." Soon the bride and groom invite their friends and relatives to join them in offering food to the monks.

Then the highly structured ceremony continues. First the bride and groom pour holy water from one small bowl to another. Then they put on two connected headbands that symbolize the unity of marriage. At the same time, the monks begin to form a circle around the guests with a long piece of

Buddhism in Thailand

The religion of Buddhism began in northern India about 2,500 years ago. A royal prince named Siddhartha Gotama was being groomed by his father to become the future king. Prince Siddhartha lived a sheltered, protected life in his father's palace and was given every convenience and comfort in order to keep him happy. One day Siddhartha persuaded one of his servants to take him on a ride around the city. On his trip outside the palace walls, Siddhartha saw four things that confused him and caused him to think differently about life: an old man, a sick man, a dying man, and a holy man.

Suddenly he was shaken out of the peace and comfort of his protected life. Prince Siddhartha decided to turn his back on comfort and follow in the footsteps of other holy men. He wanted to try to find a way to understand the nature of life and overcome suffering, greed, and desire. After his realization, called the Enlightenment, Siddhartha became known as Lord Buddha— meaning the Awakened One. His teachings, known as Buddhism, spread from India to Sri Lanka and parts of Southeast Asia, as well as to China and Japan. Buddhism is the most popular religion in Thailand.

white yarn. This is to protect everybody present from evil spirits. Finally, the bride and groom kneel together, and the monks perform the official marriage ceremony. Once they have prayed and chanted over the kneeling couple for half an hour, the religious part of the ceremony is over. Before the monks leave, they sprinkle holy water on the wedding couple and the guests.

After the monks leave, the celebration begins. The wedding party, family, and friends celebrate the joyful occasion with music, food, and drink. Later the couple visits the town or city hall to make the marriage official. The Buddhist wedding ceremony is practiced throughout Thailand—about 95 percent of Thais are Buddhists—but it is not recognized as a legal wedding.

Lunar or Solar, Chinese or Buddhist?

The Thai calendar has been adapted to the Western calendar with days, weeks, and months. Before, many Thais went by the Buddhist, or solar, calendar, which begins numbering years starting with the passing of Lord Buddha. The Western calendar begins numbering at Christ's birth, which occurred 543 years later. This means that the Western year 2009 is the year 2552 on the Buddhist calendar.

The lunar calendar, adapted from the Chinese, is based on the phases of the moon. Each moon cycle lasts 29 days, 12 hours, and 44 minutes, the exact time it takes the moon to orbit Earth. Each month begins on the first day of the new moon. The lunar calendar is used mainly for religious holidays.

CELEBRATING RELIGION AND NATION

Even though Songkran is a time of fun, the period around it is known as the "seven dangerous days." Increased traffic, intoxication, and slick roads pose a risk to celebrants—especially motorcycle drivers. More than 320 people were killed and another 4,480 were injured during the 2008 festival.

Water Festival

Like weddings, most holidays in Thailand combine serious elements of Buddhism with social fun. One of the country's biggest annual festivals is the Songkran Festival. This three-to-four-day holiday takes place in mid-April each year, marking the new year of the lunar calendar. Although Thailand has officially adopted the Western calendar, many holidays and religious celebrations still reference the traditional lunar calendar.

Throughout Thailand, Songkran is celebrated as a water festival. Pouring water is meant to wash away any bad luck for the coming year and to bring rain in coming months. Teens join the rest of their family for a ritual bathing of their elders. Usually this means that family members visit the grandparents and pour scented water on their elders' hands. Then the elders wish the young people good luck in the coming year. Next the family may visit a *wat*, or Buddhist temple. Here they show respect to Buddha by washing a statue of Buddha. Sometimes they also join in the ceremonial bathing of a monk.

The real fun for most teens at Songkran Festival is found in the streets. In many towns and cities, the streets turn into a giant water fight. People fill bowls, cups, and jars—whatever they can find—with water. Often the roads are so jammed with water-throwers that cars and motorcycles can't get through. The only thing that's certain is that everybody ends up wet.

wat
(wat)

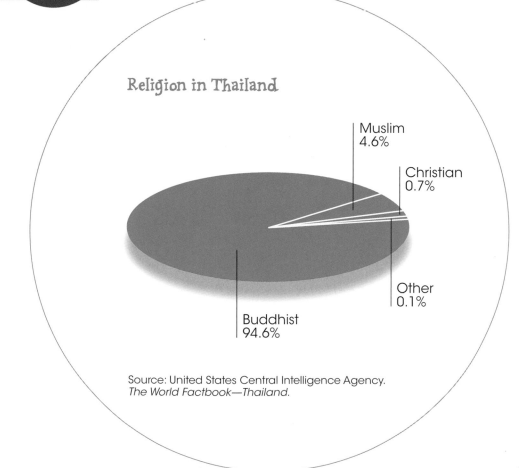

Religion in Thailand

Muslim
4.6%

Christian
0.7%

Other
0.1%

Buddhist
94.6%

Source: United States Central Intelligence Agency.
The World Factbook—Thailand.

More Buddhist Celebrations

Thai people observe several Buddhist holy days throughout the year. The most important of these is Visakha Bucha Day, or Triple Anniversary Day. It's called triple day because it marks three events in the life of Siddhartha, the man who became known as Buddha. The day marks his birth, death, and enlightenment. Unlike the boisterous fun of Songkran, Visakha Bucha Day is a sacred event. One of the best-known celebrations takes place in the city of Chiang Mai. Here the day includes a procession from the city to a famous temple that sits high on a mountain overlooking the city.

A large crowd gathers in the city and begins its 5.6-mile (9-km) journey up the winding mountain road at sunset.

Three New Year's

Along with Songkran, the traditional Thai New Year, Thai people celebrate two other New Years throughout the year. The first is January 1, the Western calendar's New Year's Day. Most Thais, along with people around the globe, celebrate New Year's Eve on December 31 with late-night parties. On New Year's Day, however, many Thais incorporate a religious aspect into their celebrations. Most Thais have the day off from work and school. Visiting temples with family and making merit is a common New Year's Day activity.

The next New Year's celebration is the Chinese New Year. The date of Chinese New Year changes each year with the lunar calendar, but it is most often celebrated in January. Since many Thais are descendents of Chinese, it's a big holiday in Thailand. Firecrackers and parades can be seen across cities and villages. Young children receive red envelopes containing money as a symbol of luck for the coming year. Teens spend the day celebrating with family or friends.

National Public Holidays

New Year's Day

January 1

Makha Bucha Day (Buddhist All Saints Day)

Moveable date in late January to early March

Chakri Day (celebration of the current dynasty)

April 6

Songkran Day (Thai New Year)

Moveable date in April

National Labor Day

May 1

Coronation Day

May 5

Visakha Bucha Day (Triple Anniversary Day)

Moveable date in May

Asalaha Bucha Day (Buddhist Monkhood Day)

Moveable date in July

Khao Phansa (beginning of Buddhist Lent)

Moveable date in July

Queen's Birthday

August 12

Chulalongkorn Day (death of King Rama V)

October 23

King's Birthday (Thailand's National Day)

December 5

Constitution Day

December 10

New Year's Eve

December 31

Celebrants usually arrive at the temple about 3 A.M. They wait until daybreak to begin paying their respects to Buddha. First they offer food to the monks who live there. The rest of the day is filled with prayers before ancient Buddhist relics at the temple, and chanting and sermons from the monks. At dusk, celebrants holding candles and joss sticks walk three times around the temple's main chapel in a final procession.

Three other Buddhist holy days are celebrated throughout Thailand. Makha Bucha Day, or All Saints Day, marks a day when an unplanned sermon by Buddha drew more than 1,350 people. During the sermon, Buddha spelled out some of his most important views on attaining enlightenment, and also foresaw his own death. Today Thai people celebrate this day when the full moon appears between late January and

The name Makha Bucha comes from the Pali words makha (the name of the third lunar month) and bucha (to worship).

early March. Similar processions take place on Asalaha Bucha Day (Buddhist Monkhood Day). This celebration in July marks the day when Buddha preached his first sermon. All three holy days include candle-lit processions around Buddhist temples.

Soon after Buddhist Monkhood Day is Khao Phansa, or the beginning of Buddhist Lent, a time for reflection and meditation lasting from late July to October. During this time, monks stay in their temples for three months. This is also the time when those wishing

Buffalo racing is a popular spectator sport during Buddhist Lent. A fast buffalo can cost as much as 800,000 baht (U.S.$23,500).

Muslims in Thailand

Nearly 5 percent of Thais are Muslim, and there are more than 3,000 registered mosques throughout the country. Most Thai Muslims live in the southern part of the country. Malaysia, which borders Thailand in the south, is a primarily Muslim country. Many Thai Muslims are of Malay descent and speak Yawi, a Malay dialect.

For years, Muslims and Buddhists coexisted in separate areas. Currently Thailand's Muslim people feel increasingly divided from the rest of the population. Several Islamic separatist groups are present in the area, and more conflicts have occurred since the September 11, 2001, attacks on the World Trade Center in New York City and other acts of global violence. It has been estimated that as many as 3,000 people have been killed and more than 6,000 violent incidents have occurred between 2004 and 2007 as a result of this religious conflict.

Nearly 80 percent of all students in southern Thailand attend religious Islamic schools.

to join monasteries do so. Buddhists around the country practice restraint and participate in merit making. They also bring offerings of food, sweets, and other useful items to the monks. Most Buddhists also fast, going without food and drink, for some period during Buddhist Lent.

National Pride

Not all of the holidays that Thai teens celebrate are Buddhist occasions. Thais also celebrate several national events throughout the year—including showing appreciation for their leaders, past and present. Thailand has a strong sense of national pride. In fact, it is the only Southeast Asian country that has never

King Bhumibol

King Bhumibol Adulyadej, also known as Rama IX, has ruled during more than a dozen military coups and outlasted 20 prime ministers. Born in 1927 in the United States, Bhumibol was pushed onto the throne at the age of 18 after his brother's death. When he married the daughter of a Thai diplomat in 1950, he was crowned monarch of the Kingdom of Thailand.

During his 80th birthday celebration, he said:

Whether soldiers or civilians, [we] must be united, like our legs that must be united—which means one goes forward and one pushes back before moving forward. ... This way, we could walk without falling. Without unity, the country will face disaster.

King Bhumibol is the world record holder for honorary university degrees and is the only Thai monarch (and possibly only monarch in the world) to hold a patent. In 2006, during the 60th anniversary of his ascension to the throne, he was awarded the United Nations' first Human Development Lifetime Achievement Award. Today he is the longest-reigning monarch in the world.

CELEBRATING RELIGION AND NATION

been a colony of a European country. Thai people are quite proud of their long history of independence.

Each year on April 6, Thai students have the day off from school and take part in a wreath-laying ceremony. They are paying respect to Thailand's previous leaders and current ruling family. The day is called Chakri Day, after the Chakri dynasty, the present-day family of kings. Thailand's King Bhumibol is the ninth ruler in the Chakri dynasty. On Chakri Day, he leads a ceremony at the Chapel Royal, home to Thailand's most sacred image of Buddha.

Coronation Day, which occurs on May 5, marks the day in 1950 that King Bhumibol took the throne. The celebration begins on May 3 and consists of a number of religious ceremonies. On

Thousands of Thais and monarchs from more than 25 countries attended the 60th anniversary of King Bhumibol's rule in 2006.

Thousands of Thais dressed in pink and yellow (colors associated with the king) traveled to the Grand Palace for Bhumibol's 80th birthday in 2007.

the first day, a Buddhist ceremony takes place at the Grand Palace. The second day consists of a two-part ceremony— one Hindu and one Buddhist. Finally, on the third day, the king makes merit and leads a ceremony at Thailand's most sacred temple, the Temple of the Emerald Buddha. It is the only Buddhist temple in Thailand without monks. People who have made important contributions to the country are also

honored on this day.

Most Thais think of King Bhumibol and his wife, Queen Sirikit, as honored elders. In fact, they celebrate their birth- days as Father's Day and Mother's Day. Teens have the day off from school and work on both December 5, the king's birthday, and August 12, the queen's birthday. On these days, families around Thailand put up elaborate decorations inside and outside their houses. Teens as

well as younger children show respect to their parents by bowing deeply before them and often presenting them with a jasmine garland.

Another royal celebration, which occurs on October 23, is Chulalongkorn Day. This important day marks the death of King Rama V (also known as Chulalongkorn) in 1910. During his 42-year reign from 1868 to 1910, King Rama V abolished slavery in Thailand.

He did much to modernize the country, establishing hospitals, medical schools, education systems, railways, and post offices. It is believed that people who pay their respects to the king are blessed with prosperity and good luck. Because of this, his picture is found in most Thai houses, and on Chulalongkorn Day, candles and wreaths are left by his statue in downtown Bangkok.

Rice is an important crop in Thailand. Between January and July 2008, the country exported more than 6 million tons (5.4 metric tons) of rice.

5

A Changing Workplace

FOR CENTURIES, MOST THAIS HAVE SUPPORTED THEMSELVES AS FARMERS OR FISHERMEN. Thai farmers have traditionally grown an abundance of crops, including rice, sugarcane, vegetables, and fruits such as bananas and mangoes. Farmers have used water buffalo—large animals with boxy hooves that help them move around in wet rice fields—to plant and cultivate rice and other crops. In southern Thailand and along its eastern coast, most people have made their living fishing for seafood—both freshwater and saltwater.

These farmers and fishermen have worked for themselves, growing or catching enough to provide for their own families. Then they have traded for items they needed, such as clothes and utensils made by craftspeople. For centuries, Thai craftspeople have been making goods such as silk clothing and rattan baskets made from the branches of native palm plants.

Like all aspects of life in Thailand, the world of work has changed dramatically as the country has become more involved in the world economy. Today fishing and

63

Lumber Work

Turning trees into lumber for ships, furniture, and other items is big business in Thailand. Northern Thailand is home to some of the most valuable trees in the world: teak trees. Teak is a hardwood with a smooth, oily surface that is ideal for both intricate carving and constructing durable outdoor goods such as ships. In fact, Thailand is one of only four countries in the world with natural teak forests.

For centuries, Thais used elephants to help cut down and gather teakwood. Today it is more commonly forested with machines in northern Thailand and then transported by river or road to sawmills in the central part of the country. These sawmills provide employment for many central Thai residents.

farming are still popular occupations. However, new technology has changed the way people work. For instance, rice farmers have begun using mechanical plows rather than water buffalo to harvest rice crops. With mechanical plows, they can plant and harvest larger crops. Fishing has also changed in recent years. Manmade freshwater farms now provide much more bounty with less effort. These new developments mean that fewer workers make more food. The extra food is exported to other countries.

Today Thailand supplies rice and fish to much of the world. Before rice or fish is exported, it needs to be processed and packaged in factories. Manufacturing is one of the fastest growing aspects of Thailand's economy. Apart from processing rice and fish, Thai factories make cars, computers, and other electronics, which are also exported around the world. As fewer Thais work in fishing and farming, more work in manufacturing as well as sales and services. These occupations, along with store and restaurant workers, bankers, and tourist workers, are necessary in an advancing society.

Jobs for Teens

Thai teens are also affected by the economic changes in their country. In the past, many teens dropped out of school to work in farming or fishing. While the work was hard and did not pay well, they had to do it to help their

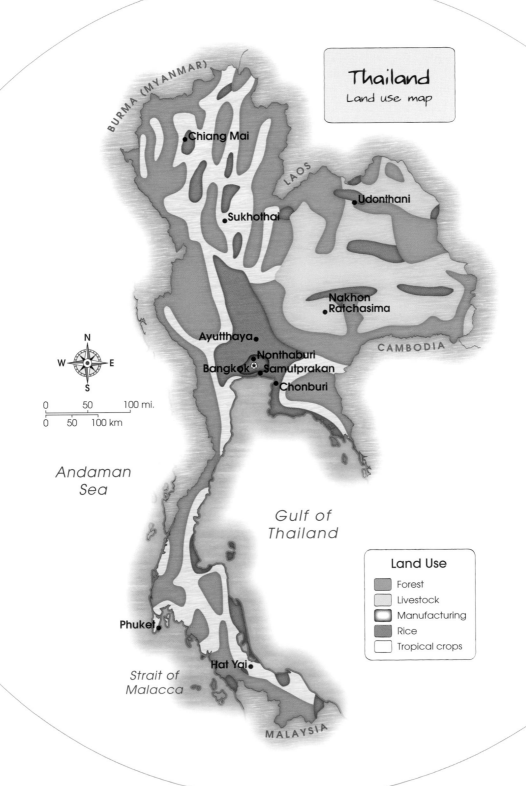

Thailand
Land use map

Chiang Mai

BURMA (MYANMAR)

LAOS

Sukhothai

Udonthani

Nakhon
Ratchasima

CAMBODIA

Ayutthaya

Nonthaburi
Bangkok Samutprakan
Chonburi

N
W E
S

0   50   100 mi.
0   50   100 km

Andaman
Sea

Gulf of
Thailand

Phuket

Strait of
Malacca

Hat Yai

MALAYSIA

Land Use
Forest
Livestock
Manufacturing
Rice
Tropical crops

families. Because they had dropped out of school, they had little chance of finding a better job later in life. In 1985, nearly 70 percent of Thai teens between the ages of 15 and 19 were employed.

Now, more than two decades later, the number of employed teens has dropped below 40 percent. This is partially because in 2001 the Thai government raised the legal working age

Teens can earn between 3,000 and 8,000 baht (U.S.$90 and $235) a month by working a part-time job.

from 13 to 15. The result is that more teenagers are staying in high school today, and fewer are dropping out to get jobs. Another reason for the drop in teenage workers is that Thailand's economy prospered during the 1990s. Businesses did very well, and jobs were easier to find. Many workers began earning higher wages than they ever had before. That meant fewer teens had to work to

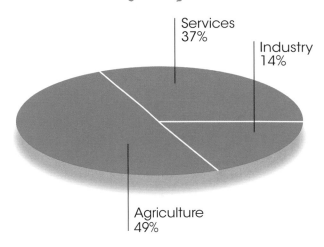

Labor Force by Occupation

Services 37%

Industry 14%

Agriculture 49%

Source: United States Central Intelligence Agency. *The World Factbook—Thailand.*

Burst Bubble

Beginning in the 1980s, Thailand's economy grew by leaps and bounds. Families that had lived off of farming for centuries began to find better paying and easier jobs. Many Thais made a lot of money during this period. They also bought many luxury items such as imported cars, new condominiums, and technology products.

In 1997, the bubble burst in the Thai economy. Many businesses and banks failed, people lost jobs, and those who were still employed could no longer afford the luxury items they had recently bought. Today Thailand continues its slow recovery from this poor economic period. It's slowly becoming easier to find jobs that pay well. And people, especially teens, are once again beginning to spend money more freely.

Tourism Jobs

Many Thai teens aspire to jobs in their country's huge tourist industry. Thailand is known around the world as an exotic vacation destination. The city of Bangkok has long been a leading tourist draw, but recently the beaches of southern Thailand have become equal attractions.

In particular, the tourist resorts on the southern island of Phuket are becoming top-notch destinations for travelers from Asia, Europe, and North America. There are plenty of jobs serving the tourists that visit Thailand. Teens can give group tours, or work in hotels or restaurants. Those who want to break into this industry need to learn one or more foreign languages, such as English, Japanese, Chinese, or European languages.

help support their families.

The kind of work that teens do has changed a great deal. Fewer teens are working on farms. In 1997, nearly 43 percent of working teens were employed in agricultural jobs. By 2005, only about 35 percent were doing farm work. Meanwhile, more and more teens were finding work in factories, stores, and restaurants. Many working teens are still in school, working parttime while they finish their education. This means they will have the chance to get a better job and earn more money when they are older.

Why Work?

The reasons Thai teens work have changed in recent years. In previous generations, Thai teens worked because they needed to help support their families. To some degree, this is still true. Teens who live in poorer regions, such as the northern hill area, are more likely to drop out of school early to take low-wage jobs that will help support their families. They earn money by selling food or other items at roadside stalls, or take unskilled construction or other low-wage jobs.

Most middle- and upper-income teens do not need to earn money to support their families. They are more likely to graduate from high school and go on to college. They take a part-time job only to support their own spending habits. These habits can be expensive. Keeping up with pop culture and fashion

Pantip Plaza in Bangkok has hundreds of stores devoted to technology. Many shoppers are interested in the wide range of pirated software and secondhand computer equipment carried by the stores.

is important to those living in the city. They buy imported clothes and music and spend money—sometimes *lots* of money—on cell phones. They need plenty of cash to support their daily phone habits. As one teen explained,

Without my mobile phone, my life is nothing. … I need it to contact my friends, like, where we should meet in the morning or where to meet in the

evening for tutoring courses. The cell phone is very important. For example, if I am on the bus and I want to call friends out for a movie, I can call their cell phones without having to call them at home and ask for their parents' permission.

Some teens spend as much as 8,000 baht (U.S.$235) per month—about the same as the average monthly pay in Thailand—on their phone bill. Sometimes parents will pay it, but if they don't, teens might have to give up entertainment or fast food, or even get a job, to pay their phone bills.

Trouble Finding Work

Although Thai teens today have many more career choices, they still face problems finding a job. Overall, Thailand has a low unemployment rate

Catering to tourists is one way teens make extra money.

of about 1.7 percent. But for teens, the unemployment rate is around 5 percent. Almost one-half of all unemployed people in Thailand are between the ages of 15 and 24.

It can be particularly hard for college and high school graduates to find good jobs. Sometimes this is because schools may not teach the technical skills they need. As the nature of work in Thailand has changed, the types of abilities that workers need have also changed. Even though Thai youth tend to stay in school longer today than in the past, some people say they are not learning the skills they need for Thailand's new jobs. This may be why the unemployment rate is so much higher for young people than for older people.

Sometimes Thai teens and young college graduates don't find good jobs because they don't know where to look. Schools in Thailand do not usually have career centers to help students find jobs. In fact, close to 65 percent of Thais rely on their parents or immediate relatives to find employment. About 22 percent get help from their teachers or other close adults. Only 13 percent find work through job announcements or by contacting an employer they don't know.

Spending Money

According to a survey, 52 percent of urban Thai teens ages 13 to 18 have part-time jobs. Around 30 percent earn an average of 1,970 baht (U.S.$58) a month, and 25 percent earn about 850 baht (U.S.$25) a month. The average income for an adult working a full-time job is 12,500 baht (U.S.$370) a month. One survey's findings found that:

Thai teenagers are not pessimistic about the economic turmoil and have a strong confidence that Thailand will again become economically successful.

While they may be impressed with American style or Japanese technology, Thai teens prefer to show their loyalties by buying Thai.

71

Thais take their football (soccer) seriously. So seriously, in fact, that a golden statue of soccer star David Beckham has been enshrined in a temple near Bangkok.

6 Hanging Out and Having Fun

IT'S GETTING LATE IN THE EVENING, BUT THE SUN IS STILL SHINING ON A MAKE-SHIFT SOCCER FIELD IN CENTRAL THAILAND. It's mid-April—the height of the hot season—and the temperature is close to 95 F (35 C). Athletes who gathered for this informal game of football (soccer) don't seem to notice the heat. Some have taken off their shirts, but many more wear T-shirts or jerseys from their favorite European, Asian, or Latin American teams. By far, the most popular shirt is the red Manchester United home-game shirt, the same style of jersey worn by one of the world's most popular teams.

The game of football is wildly popular across Thailand. Teens love to get together for informal games or play in competition for one of the country's many football leagues. Many also follow their favorite teams in international competition. Thailand has women's and men's national football teams that play around the world. Every four years, Thailand competes in the Asian Cup against 15 other countries, including Iran, China, Korea, and Saudi Arabia.

Most Thai teens say that football is their favorite sport, but it's certainly not the only popular sport in Thailand. In school and out, Thai teens play other Western sports such as basketball, baseball, and volleyball. Another common sport, called *takraw* came to Thailand from neighboring Burma (Myanmar).

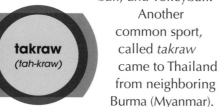

takraw
(tah-kraw)

Takraw is similar to volleyball, but the players use their feet instead of their hands, and there are only three members to a team. It's often played on a basketball court with a net stretched across the middle. The players kick the woven wicker ball back and forth across the net; a team scores when the other team lets the ball touch the ground. Takraw is an easy game to play because it doesn't require too many players or special equipment.

The modern version of takraw began taking shape in the early 1740s. The first public competition took place in 1870.

Thai teens also like to watch sports. Of course football and basketball are popular spectator sports, but the sport with the biggest spectator draw in Thailand is the national sport, *Muay Thai*, or Thai kickboxing. It is also called the science of eight limbs, because Thai boxers use

Muay Thai
(my-tie)

eight contact spots to strike opponents: both shins, both hands, both elbows, and both knees. Points are given for each strike, and a round ends when one boxer earns 10 points. The art of Muay Thai has been around for hundreds of years and remains popular throughout Thailand. In Bangkok, teens go with their families and friends to watch Muay Thai at the Rajadamnern Boxing Stadium.

Got Game?

Computer games are immensely popular with Thai teens. Nearly 95 percent of teens play computer games regularly. Students say they spend an average of one to two hours each weekday playing computer games, and three to four hours per day on the weekends. During school holidays, students report spending up to five hours a day gaming.

More than 700,000 young Thais play Ragnarok Online, a multiplayer role-playing game. After concerns were raised about players not getting enough sleep, the Thai government implemented a 10 P.M. curfew on players under 18—older players had to register for an adult user I.D. that allowed them to play later. A government official said:

In the developed countries or in the Western countries, parents have enough time to look after their children. ... But in the developing world, in Thailand, the parents, especially those parents who have teenage children, they must work very hard and they work until very late at night so they don't have the time to look after their children properly.

Music Scene

Thai youth are also passionate about music. They listen to pop music by Thai bands and solo musicians, as well as imports from around the world. Teens buy CDs, download music onto their personal music players, hear their favorite bands on the radio, and watch videos on the 24-hour MTV Thailand television channel. Teens also listen to traditional Thai music at home, at festivals, and at other events.

Urban teens have the most opportunities to see their favorite bands live. On a typical evening inside a local Bangkok club, teens might find one of

MP3 players are one of the fastest-selling products in Thailand.

the country's hottest bands—Clash—on stage. Lead singer Bank is wearing a black kerchief tied around his head and an oversized, bright red T-shirt with the sleeves ripped off. His bandmates—Ponn and Hack on guitar, Soom on bass, and Yak on drums—are similarly dressed in pop grunge style. The crowd is hot and sweaty, and they clamor to get close to the stage. Clash's top hits include "Thu Cha Yu Kap Chan Talot Pai" ("You Will Be With Me Forever") and "Thu Khu Nangfa Nai Chai" ("You Are the Angel in My Heart"). They've been at the top of the Thai music charts since their debut album in 2001. Although their name is an English word, they sing in Thai. Other top Thai bands also have English names such as Silly Fools and Bodyslam.

As much as teens like their own Thai bands, they don't limit themselves to local music. MTV Thailand is full of just about every version of pop music from around the world. J-pop (Japanese pop music) and K-pop (Korean pop music) are huge, but the country is also full of fans of punk rock, heavy metal, Latin pop, hip-hop, and techno pop. In short, Thai teens have grown up in a culture where music is incorporated into every aspect of social life. Most gatherings—from huge festivals to small family events—feature music, and joining right in is part of the fun. If no one has an instrument, groups will break into spontaneous sing-alongs. Most restaurants cater to Thais' love of music by placing karaoke machines prominently in their dining rooms. A night out at a local karaoke bar is considered fun for Thais of all ages.

Thailand has a long history of music. Over the centuries, it has borrowed from the musical styles of many of its neighbors, including China and India. Thai classical music is famous for

On The Screen

Television and movies are a big part of teen life in Thailand. Many soap-opera-style television shows called *lakhon* attract huge audiences. One of the most famous people in Thailand is actress Anne Thongprasom, who is best known for her leading role in the television show *The Letter: Chotmai Rak.*

lakhon
(la-corn)

77

The word *jakhae* comes from the Thai word for crocodile—the animal that the instrument resembles.

its large orchestras featuring percussion and string and wind instruments. Many of these instruments are borrowed—such as the *khim*, a Chinese dulcimer, and the *jakhae*, a string instrument. The style is more than 800 years old and was perfected by playing it before generations of Thai royalty.

khim
(kim)

jakhae
(jak-hay)

A more recent Thai music style is *Luk thung*, or Thai country music, most well-known in rural areas. Its lyrics typically describe the hardships faced by farmers and other rural residents, and it has been compared to country western music in the United States. In north-

Luk thung
(look-thoong)

eastern Thailand, another style of folk music called *Molam* is popular. Molam, which originated in the neighboring country of Laos, is similar to Luk thung and features lyrics about rural life. Today many teens in northeastern Thailand listen to a modern version of Molam, called *Molam Sing*.

Molam
(maw-lum)

Molam Sing
(maw-lum sing)

On the Street

A quick glance down a city street or village road shows that rural and urban Thai teens have quite different cultural influences. Rural teens may listen to CDs by trendy Thai and foreign pop musicians or have T-shirts emblazoned with images of their favorite pop star. But for the most part, rural teens are tuned in to their village and family lives.

Thai urban teens, on the other hand, are tuned in to a wide range of

Many local fashion designers are tuned in to the latest trends.

pop culture influences. On any city street are stores displaying the latest fashions, brand-name products, and trendy devices such as mobile phones and personal music players from around the world. Billboards and video screens flash images of the latest pop culture icons from Japan, Korea, Europe, and the United States. Teens clog the most popular streets in Bangkok, spending money on the latest styles in hair, fashion, jewelry, and music. In Bangkok, body piercing and extreme haircuts and hair colors are all the rage.

Teens also love hanging out with their friends at night and experiencing the vibrant nightlife of the city. Live bands or karaoke music can be found seven nights a week in Bangkok. One survey found that about 40 percent of urban teens spend between 3,000 and 6,000 baht (U.S.$90 and $175) a month on nightlife. Bangkok also has a thriving illegal drug culture. Many Thai

At the Beach

With its tropical climate and miles of coastline, Thailand is home to some of the world's most beautiful white-sand beaches. Some areas in southern Thailand, such as the island of Phuket, have been top international beach destinations for several decades. Other beaches that are easier to access from Bangkok are popular family vacation destinations. Bangkok families often spend a week at resorts in Pattaya and Bangsaen, which are short drives from the capital city. For long weekends, families head to the beaches in Rayong province.

In December 2004, hundreds of miles of Thailand's beautiful beaches were devastated by the tsunami that struck southern Thailand. In the aftermath of the destruction, rebuilding the beaches and resorts was not as important as helping people in more immediate danger. Restoring the beaches and the tourist industry that depends on them is a goal of the Thai government. Slowly, the natural beauty and vacation atmosphere of southern Thailand is returning.

teens are tempted by the lure of illegal drugs before they realize how easily drugs can destroy their lives. The Thai government has many programs aimed at keeping teens away from drugs.

In fact, many adults in Thailand worry that teens are too obsessed with pop culture and spending money on the latest fashion trends. They worry that this can take away from traditional Thai values and perhaps lead to involvement in drugs. Some surveys show that adults may be worrying too much. In a survey of 1,200 Thai teens, most of the teens said that they hold on to many traditional Thai values. They agree that children should be responsible for taking care of their parents, and they say that their parents are the people who understand them best. According to the teens, the top five challenging issues facing Thailand today are drugs, the economy, the environment, traffic problems, and the loss of Thai identity.

Faced with technology, Western fashion, and modern ways, teens make a point to hang onto their Thai roots.

Looking Ahead

TEENS IN THAILAND LIVE IN A RAPIDLY CHANGING WORLD. THEIR COUNTRY HAS A LONG, PROUD HISTORY. It has also seen recent explosive and exciting developments. For centuries, Thailand thrived as a rural farming-based society. Today global trade, tourism, and modern technology have transformed Bangkok and other Thai cities into international urban centers. Thai teens live in a world that is quite different, not only from the world of their ancestors but also from the world of their parents.

The social and economic changes that today's Thai teens are experiencing give them more choices than their parents had. This modern situation also requires them to balance their cultural traditions with modern values.

Most teens have embraced the changes brought about by technology and globalism. They are likely to have computers, cell phones, and personal music players. They are also aware that some of these changes threaten the well-being of their country. Increased pollution from Bangkok's world-famous traffic congestion is just one of the negative impacts of modernization. The challenge for Thai teens in the future will be to help their country modernize while holding on to their culture's healthy values.

Official name: Kingdom of Thailand

Capital: Bangkok

People

Population: 65,068,149

Population by age group:
0–14 years: 21.2%
15–64 years: 70.3%
65 years and over: 8.5%

Life expectancy at birth: 73 years

Official language: Thai

Other common languages: English (secondary language of the elite), ethnic and regional dialects

Religion:
Buddhist: 94.6%
Muslim: 4.6%
Christian: 0.7%
Other: 0.1%

Legal ages
Alcohol consumption: 20
Driver's license: car: 18; motorcycle: 15
Employment: 15
Leave school: 16
Marriage: 15
Military service: 18 for voluntary service;
at age 21 all males serve two years of
mandatory military service
Voting: 18

Government

Type of government: Constitutional monarchy

Chief of state: King

Head of government: Prime minister

Lawmaking body: Bicameral National Assembly composed of the Senate and the House of Representatives

Administrative divisions: 76 provinces

Independence: Only Southeast Asian nation never under colonial rule. Unified Thai kingdom established in mid-14th century; known as Siam until 1939

National symbol: The elephant symbolizes power, honor, and peace. The flag has five horizontal bands of red, white, blue (double width), white, and red

Geography

Total area: 205,600 square miles (514,000 square kilometers)

Climate: tropical; rainy, warm, cloudy southwest monsoon (mid-May to September); dry, cool northeast monsoon (November to mid-March); southern isthmus always hot and humid

Highest point: Doi Inthanon, 8,500 feet (2,576 meters)

Lowest point: Gulf of Thailand, sea level

Major rivers: Chi, Mun, Nan, Chao Phraya, and Mekong

Major landforms: Highest peaks: Doi Inthanon, Doi Luang, and Phu Soi Dao; Islands: Phuket, Koh Samui, and Koh Chang

Economy

Currency: Baht

Population below poverty line: 10%

Major natural resources: tin, rubber, natural gas, tungsten, tantalum, timber, lead, fish, gypsum, lignite, fluorite, arable land

Major agricultural products: rice, cassava (tapioca), rubber, corn, sugarcane, coconuts, soybeans

Major exports: textiles, footwear, fishery products, rice, rubber, jewelry, automobiles, computers, electrical appliances

Major imports: capital goods, intermediate goods and raw materials, consumer goods, fuels

Historical Timeline

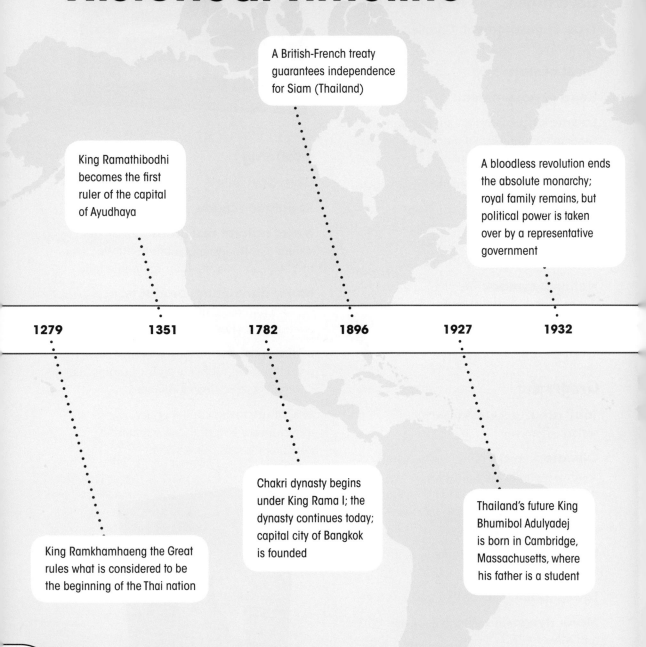

A British-French treaty guarantees independence for Siam (Thailand)

King Ramathibodhi becomes the first ruler of the capital of Ayudhaya

A bloodless revolution ends the absolute monarchy; royal family remains, but political power is taken over by a representative government

1279   **1351**   **1782**   **1896**   **1927**   **1932**

Chakri dynasty begins under King Rama I; the dynasty continues today; capital city of Bangkok is founded

Thailand's future King Bhumibol Adulyadej is born in Cambridge, Massachusetts, where his father is a student

King Ramkhamhaeng the Great rules what is considered to be the beginning of the Thai nation

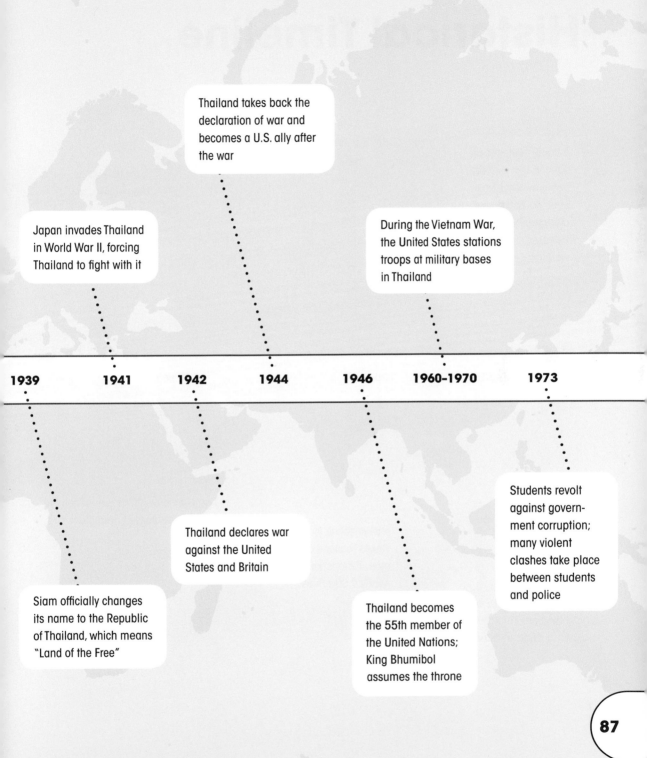

Thailand takes back the declaration of war and becomes a U.S. ally after the war

Japan invades Thailand in World War II, forcing Thailand to fight with it

During the Vietnam War, the United States stations troops at military bases in Thailand

| 1939 | 1941 | 1942 | 1944 | 1946 | 1960–1970 | 1973 |

Students revolt against govern-ment corruption; many violent clashes take place between students and police

Thailand declares war against the United States and Britain

Siam officially changes its name to the Republic of Thailand, which means "Land of the Free"

Thailand becomes the 55th member of the United Nations; King Bhumibol assumes the throne

Historical Timeline

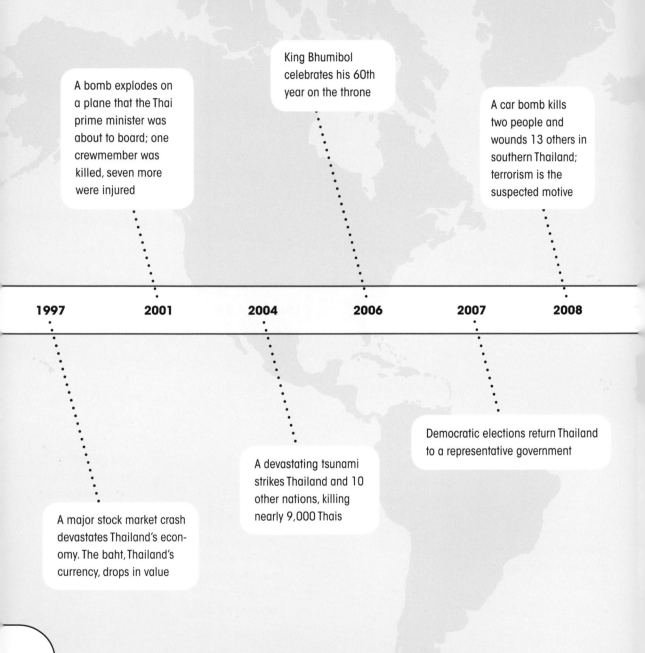

A bomb explodes on a plane that the Thai prime minister was about to board; one crewmember was killed, seven more were injured

King Bhumibol celebrates his 60th year on the throne

A car bomb kills two people and wounds 13 others in southern Thailand; terrorism is the suspected motive

1997   **2001**   **2004**   **2006**   **2007**   **2008**

Democratic elections return Thailand to a representative government

A devastating tsunami strikes Thailand and 10 other nations, killing nearly 9,000 Thais

A major stock market crash devastates Thailand's economy. The baht, Thailand's currency, drops in value

Glossary

coup	sudden change of government, often by force
dowry	property that a woman brings to her husband in marriage
economy	the way a country produces, distributes, and uses its money, goods, natural resources, and services
Islam	religion founded on the Arabian Peninsula in the seventh century by the prophet Muhammad
joss stick	type of incense often burned in Buddhist ceremonies
longan	fruit tree native to Southeast Asia
monsoon	weather season characterized by very heavy rainfall
mosque	Islamic place of worship
Muslim	religious follower of Islam, or referring to a follower of Islam
nuclear family	family group that consists of a father, mother, and children
procession	number of people walking or driving along a route as part of a public festival or religious ceremony
separatist	person who chooses to separate or break away from an established church or nation
tsunami	gigantic ocean wave created by an undersea earthquake, landslide, or volcanic eruption

Additional Resources

FURTHER READING

Fiction and nonfiction titles to enhance your introduction to teens in Thailand, past and present.

Ho, Minfong. *Rice Without Rain*. New York: William Morrow and Co., 1990.

Winther, Barbara. *Plays From Asian Tales: India, Burma, Thailand, Vietnam*. Studio City, Calif.: Players Press, 2004.

Collins, Paul. *Muay Thai: Thai Boxing*. New York: Chelsea House Publications, 2001.

Phillips, Douglas A., and Charles F. Gritzner. *Thailand*. New York: Chelsea House Publications, 2007.

Taus-Bolstad, Stacy. *Thailand in Pictures*. Minneapolis: Lerner Publications, 2003.

ON THE WEB

For more information on this topic, use FactHound.

1. Go to www.facthound.com
2. Choose your grade level.
3. Begin your search.

This book's ID number is 9780756540463
FactHound will find the best sites for you.

Source Notes

Page 16, sidebar, column 1, line 1: Sriwittayapaknam School. "Scout Promise." Scouting in Thailand. 28 July 2008. www.thaiscouting.com/scouting.html

Page 35, column 2, line 19: Panrit "Gor" Daoruang. "Fast Food Restaurants in Thailand." Thailand Life. January 2001. 29 July 2008. www.thailandlife.com/1997-2001/fast-food-restaurants-in-thailand.html

Page 40, column 2, line 14: Neil Stoneham. "Teenage Kicks." Learning Post. 8 Feb. 2005. 15 July 2008. www.bangkokpost.com/education/site2005/cvfb0805.htm

Page 58, sidebar, column 1, line 13: "Thais Mark King's 80th Birthday." BBC News. 5 Dec. 2007. 14 July 2008. http://news.bbc.co.uk/2/hi/asia-pacific/7128105.stm

Page 69, column 1, line 7: Mukdawan Sakboon. "The Essential Device: Life in the Phone Lane." *The Nation.* 24 May 2002. 5 July 2008. www.thailandlife.com/thaiyouth_75.html

Page 71, sidebar, column 2, line 1: Kwanchai Rungfapaisarn. "Thai Teenagers More Careful About Money." *The Nation.* 24 Sept. 1999. 26 July 2008. www.thailandlife.com/thaiyouth_12.html

Page 75, sidebar, column 2, line 6: "Thai Gamers Soak Up Computer Skills." BBC News. 25 Nov. 2003. 14 July 2008. http://news.bbc.co.uk/2/hi/technology/3235852.stm

Pages 84–85, At a Glance: United States Central Intelligence Agency. *The World Factbook—Thailand.* 24 July 2008. 30 July 2008. https://www.cia.gov/library/publications/the-world-factbook/geos/th.html

Select Bibliography

Brunn, Stanley D., Jack F. Williams, and Donald J. Zeigler, Eds. *Cities of the World: World Regional Urban Development (3rd edition)*. Lanham, Md.: Rowman and Littlefield, 2003.

"Crackdown on Fake Braces Fashion Fad: Thai Authorities Will Fine, Imprison Sellers of Fake Orthodontics." *CBS News*. 26 Jan. 2006. 12 March 2008. www.cbsnews.com/stories/2006/01/26/world/main1240516.shtml

"Dekoden: The Next Big Thing?" *ThaiAsiaToday.com*. 2007. 4 March 2008. www.thaiasiatoday.com/index.php?option=com_content&task=view&id=290&Itemid=105

Fuller, Thomas. "In Thai Cultural Battle, Name-Calling Is Encouraged." *The New York Times*. 29 Aug. 2007. 10 March 2008. www.nytimes.com/2007/08/29/world/asia/29nickname.html

Handley, Paul M. *The King Never Smiles*. New Haven, Conn.: Yale University Press, 2006.

Library of Congress, Federal Research Division. "*Country Profile: Thailand.*" July 2007. 14 Feb. 2008. http://lcweb2.loc.gov/frd/cs/profiles/Thailand.pdf

Sedgwick, Robert. "Education in Thailand." *World Education News & Reviews 18.2 (March/April 2005)*. 20 Feb. 2008. www.wes.org/ewenr/05mar/practical.htm

"Serious Side to Your Average Teen." *The Nation* (Bangkok). 18 Sept. 2002. 10 March 2008. www.thailandlife.com/thaiyouth_79.htm

"Thai-ing the Knot: Then & Now Marriage Customs in Central Thailand." *Welcome to Chiangmai and Chiangrai Magazine*, 2006. 24 Feb. 2008. www.chiangmai-chiangrai.com/thai_marriage2.html

Thailand Life. 16 Feb. 2008. www.thailandlife.com/1997-2001/timetable-for-junior-high.html

UNICEF. "Thailand: Statistics." 16 Feb. 2008. 29 July 2008. www.unicef.org/infobycountry/Thailand_statistics.html

United Nations Economic and Social Commission for Asia and the Pacific (UNESCAP). "Youth in Thailand: A Review of the Youth Situation and National Policies and Programmes." New York: United Nations, 2000.

U.S. Central Intelligence Agency. "Thailand." *The World Factbook*. March 2008. 21 March 2008. https://www.cia.gov/library/publications/the-world-factbook/geos/th.html

World Bank. "Thailand Social Monitor on Youth. Development and the Next Generation." January 2008. 11 March 2008. www-wds.worldbank.org/external/default/WDSContentServer/WDSP/IB/2008/03/10/000020953_20080310112731/Rendered/PDF/428520P09721301WB1SMY20081080305web.pdf

"Younger Generation Toeing the Modern Moral Line." *The Nation* (Bangkok). 3 Feb. 2008. 12 March 2008. www.nation-multimedia.com/2008/02/03/national/national_30064231.php

Index

About the Author
Sandy Donovan

Sandy Donovan has written several books for young readers about history, economics, government, and other topics. She has also worked as a newspaper reporter, a magazine editor, and a Web site developer. She has a bachelor's degree in journalism and a master's degree in public policy, and lives in Minneapolis, Minnesota, with her husband and two sons.

About the Content Adviser
Grant Olson

Grant Olson spent three years in the Peace Corps in Thailand from 1978 to 1981. Graduate studies brought him to the East-West Center and the University of Hawaii for a master's degree in Asian religions. Olson completed a Ph.D. in cultural anthropology and Southeast Asian studies at Cornell University. He remains a student of Southeast Asian culture.